the mezze
COOKBOOK

the mezze
COOKBOOK

Maria Khalifé

NEW
HOLLAND

First published in 2008 by New Holland Publishers (UK) Ltd
London • Cape Town • Sydney • Auckland

Garfield House	80 McKenzie Street	Unit 1	218 Lake Road
86–88 Edgware Road	Cape Town 8001	66 Gibbes Street	Northcote
London W2 2EA	South Africa	Chatswood	Auckland
United Kingdom		NSW 2067	New Zealand
		Australia	

1 3 5 7 9 10 8 6 4 2

ISBN   978 1 84537 978 0

Senior Editor: Corinne Masciocchi
Design: Pascal Thivillon
Jacket design: Corinne Masciocchi
Photography: Stuart West
Food styling: Stella Murphy
Editorial Direction: Rosemary Wilkinson
Production: Hema Gohil

Reproduction by Colour Scan Overseas, Singapore
Printed and bound by Times Offset (M) Bhd Sdn, Malaysia

The publishers would like to thank Denby
for the use of tableware in this book.

Contents

Introduction

The history of mezze is steeped in the Greek, Turkish and Middle Eastern cultures, and is something I feel very passionate about, having grown up with mezze as an integral part of my family's meals.

The concept of mezze came about a few centuries ago when the men arrived home in the late afternoon after a hard day's work. They would sit outside their houses enjoying small tasty dishes accompanied by a drink while socialising with friends and neighbours. The dishes were always pre-prepared, allowing wives the time to spend indoors preparing the main evening meal.

This way of sharing food and drink without any ceremony or service was a form of bonding enjoyed by cultures in bygone times, and to my great delight mezze continues to grow in popularity with today's generation and I hope generations to come.

I had the pleasure, while researching the many delicious recipes for this book, to meet with my good friend, Andonis Panayotopoulos, the Chairman of the Greek Academy of Taste. He proved to be a wonderful source of inspiration for the Greek selection of recipes and is a committed supporter of mezze. In fact, at all official functions the academy serves between eight and 10 dishes with three to four distillates so the group can enjoy socialising before the main meal is served.

I also had expert advice on Turkish dishes from my good friends Hasan Açanal and Guzin Yalin, both experts in food communications and board members at the Conservatoire International des Cuisines Mediterranéennes.

Traditionally, a variety of mezze dishes is served with a drink before the main meal, offering friends and family the opportunity to socialise and unwind after a busy day. Featuring over 90 recipes, I'm sure you will enjoy selecting from the book a wonderful array of dishes time and again for your friends and family to share. The recipes are divided into four chapters – hot and cold mezze, salads and pastries, along with a glossary of terms – and the majority of ingredients are widely available.

Throughout my years as producer of Soufra Daimeh, a widely broadcast TV food show attracting over one million viewers, magazine editor and author of the best-selling and award-winning Middle Eastern Cookbook, I have been blessed with a passion to discover the most delicious recipes in this region. As you can imagine it was a delight to work on this book, selecting dishes from across Greece, Turkey and Lebanon which are as loved today as they were centuries ago.

I hope you'll enjoy discovering the rich variety of tastes and textures within these pages which have been lovingly selected for your enjoyment.

Bon appetit, or as we like to say in Lebanon, soufra daimeh!

Glossary

In this section you will find an A to Z guide to some of the most commonly featured herbs, spices, meats, vegetables, dairy products and pulses, along with tips on how to cook them and which dishes they complement.

Aubergine Also known as eggplant, this smooth-skinned, shiny fruit comes in a variety of colours, including white, green, pink, blue-black, black and most commonly dark purple. Look for unblemished fruit, which are heavy for their size. Most aubergines do not have bitter juices, but if they do, the fruit can be sliced, sprinkled with salt and left to stand for 30 minutes to extract them. Rinse and pat dry.

Basil Large, fleshy leaves, particularly popular in Italian dishes such as pesto, basil marries well with tomatoes. To preserve the bright green or purple colour of the leaves, do not chop the leaves with a knife, but tear by hand. Use the leaves only. The purple variety has a stronger taste so less is needed.

Beetroot In past times, beetroot was cultivated for its leaves only, but these days the bulb, with its high sugar content, is the more valuable part. The most famous

usage is in borscht, although beetroot is frequently used as a vegetable and in salads. Cook without trimming, so the colour does not 'bleed'.

Broad beans Also known as fava, feves, Windsor beans and horse beans. These are oval-shaped with a thick skin. The nutty flavour and creamy texture make them especially favoured in Middle Eastern and Mediterranean cuisines.

Burghul Wheat grains which are hulled and steamed before cracking, then dried. Popular in Middle Eastern cuisine, especially vegetarian dishes, such as tabouleh.

Cabbage Related to broccoli, cauliflower, kohlrabi and Brussels sprouts. Choose heads which are heavy for their size, with crisp, shiny outer leaves. Eat raw in salads or cook for a minimum time in a covered saucepan and drain well.

Chickpeas Also known as ceci and garbanzo beans. Medium-size peas with a small pointed top. Robust and nutty flavoured, chickpeas hold their shape well with cooking. Soak chickpeas overnight in water before use, then cook for approximately 1 hour.

Cloves Cloves lose their potency after prolonged storage. To perform a freshness test, drop a clove in cold water – if fresh, it will either sink or float upright; if stale it will lie flat on the surface. Use whole or ground in meat and marinated fish dishes, pastries and mulled wine.

Coriander Sometimes called cilantro, the leaf has a distinctive aroma. It is used extensively in Mediterranean, Latin American and Asian cooking. People either love or hate this herb with a passion! The roots and leaves are a must in Thai green curry. Coriander seeds can also be used; these have a lemony flavour when crushed and can also be ground.

Cumin Without it, Middle Eastern and Latin American food would be dull. It is a popular flavouring in Indonesian cuisine and is nearly always present in curry powder. Dried cumin is often used in fruit chutneys.

Dandelion (chicory) After discarding the tough stems, the leaves are used as a salad ingredient or cooked as a vegetable side dish. The pleasantly bitter leaves should be briefly blanched before using in a salad or cooked until tender in water.

Dibs el rouman (pomegranate paste) Commonly used as a flavouring in Middle Eastern cooking, this paste is used to enhance both sweet and savoury dishes to impart a rich, complex flavour.

Dill Light green and feathery with tiny greeny-yellow flowers. This herb is used in fish and egg dishes, or finely chopped in salads. Especially good with cucumber or cottage cheese.

Dolmades An Arabic term meaning 'something stuffed', dolmades are vine (grape) leaf parcels and can be made with a number of different fillings, such as rice, meat and vegetables.

Dry yeast A leavening agent which produces carbon dioxide by fermenting sugars. Used to make breads and cake rise. Store in a cool, dry, dark place.

Feta cheese A traditional Greek cheese usually made from sheep's milk but can also be made from cow or goat's milk. It has a salty taste and crumbly texture and is a wonderful addition to salads.

Garlic Garlic is used with almost any savoury foods. Its flavour depends on how it is prepared – cooked garlic being much milder than raw, chopped garlic. It can be used raw or fried, poached, roasted or sautéed, and can be cooked peeled or unpeeled. Choose a firm, hard head of garlic with no soft or discoloured patches. Do not refrigerate but store in a cool, dry place.

Ghee A clarified butter or pure butter fat that can be heated to a high temperature without burning.

Predominantly used in Indian cooking, ghee has a long shelf life.

Halloumi cheese Traditionally made with sheep or goat's milk but now more often made with cow's milk. Similar to mozzarella, this cheese has a rubbery texture and 'squeaks' when eaten. It can be fried or grilled and goes well in salads or as an appetizer.

Kaskaval cheese Traditionally a Bulgarian sheep's milk cheese similar to Greek Kasseri cheese, it also has a strong history in Turkey. A dense cheese with a yellow colour and strong, biting taste.

Kasseri cheese A Greek cheese made from goat or sheep's milk with a hard texture and sharp, salty flavour. Good for cooking and grating over hot dishes.

Lentils Flat, lens-shaped legume, red or green to brown in colour. High in protein, lentils are full-flavoured and are commonly used in soups, stews and rice dishes. Cooking time varies depending on variety and can take 20, 40 or 60 minutes.

Makanek (sausage) Originating in Lebanon, makanek is a thin sausage made from pork or beef, and spiced with red and black pepper.

Millet A nutritious, easily digestible grain that can be used as a thickener when added to soups. Also used to make bread.

Mint Use fresh sprigs in drinks, and chopped leaves with lamb, vegetables (especially new potatoes and peas) and in fruit salads or to make a mint sauce.

Myzithra cheese Also known as Mitzithra, it is a Greek cheese made of ewe's milk, available both fresh when it is similar to cottage cheese, and aged when it is firm and strong and is ideal for grating.

Oregano An aromatic herb frequently used in Italian cooking, it can be used fresh or dried and goes well in tomato-based sauces and for seasoning meat.

Paprika Varying from mild to strong, this spice is mainly used to add flavour and colour to cooking and is made from drying sweet red peppers and then grinding them into a rich, red powder. Great in stews and vegetable dishes.

Parsley Probably the most familiar variety of culinary herb, it is hardy and highly nutritious. There are two types: curly-leaf parsley has bright green, tightly-curled leaves and is used primarily as a garnish; flat-leaf parsley has a stronger flavour and is preferred for cooking.

Finely chopped parsley leaves are amongst the mix in 'fines herbes' and the stalks are used in bouquet garni.

Pine nuts Also known as pine kernels, these are the edible seeds from pine trees. Oily and rich in protein, they are used in savoury dishes and should be kept refrigerated.

Pitta bread A versatile flat bread that can be split in half to create a pocket. It is very popular in Turkey, Greece and the Middle East, and is especially good with dips or stuffed with various fillings.

Soujouk (hot sausage) A large sausage made with minced pork or beef and pancetta popular from the Balkans to the Middle East. Some sausages are highly spiced and others seasoned with herbs and garlic.

Sumac The dried berries of this Mediterranean shrub are ground into a reddish-purplish powder. Available in local Lebanese and Middle Eastern food stores, sumac is used to infuse a dish with lemon flavour, without adding any liquid and is sprinkled on fattoush.

Swiss chard Sometimes confused with spinach, it is also known as silver beet. The leaves should be dark green and shiny and the stems white, without signs of bruising. Use the leaves cooked as you would spinach,

or raw, mixed with other salad greens. Use the stems in soups or stews, or braise them until tender, then bake in a gratin dish with Parmesan cheese.

Tahini Made from ground sesame seeds, tahini is a smooth paste with a high calcium content, particularly when the seeds have not been crushed. It is used commonly in Middle Eastern cuisines. Use in salads, humous and baba ganoush, and also as a sauce or in cakes.

Thyme A versatile herb, it has strong, aromatic leaves that are used in soups, stews, bean dishes or meat of any kind, including terrines and pâtés. Also good with vegetables, particularly roast potatoes.

Yoghurt Made from either cow's or sheep's milk, it can contain living bacteria and must be refrigerated and consumed by the 'use by' date. Available in a number of styles, it can contain up to 10.5 per cent fat.

Za'atar A group of herbs and a Middle Eastern spice blend containing sumac, sesame and marjoram. These fresh herbs are available only around the Mediterranean. Local Lebanese and Middle Eastern shops sell the spice blend, which is sprinkled on dishes including meats, vegetables and cheeses before baking. Good with barbecued meat.

Cold mezze

Aubergines stuffed with vegetables

Batinjan mahchi bil khoudar

SERVES 5
COOKING TIME: 1 HOUR 15 MINUTES

1 kg (2 lb 3 oz) short, thin aubergines
200 ml (7 fl oz) water
1½ Tbsp tomato paste
Pinch of salt

For the stuffing
Bunch of parsley, finely chopped
75 ml (2½ fl oz) olive oil
4 large tomatoes, cubed
50 ml (1¾ fl oz) lemon juice
150 g (5½ oz) small-grain white rice
2 small onions, peeled and chopped
Pinch of salt and white pepper

1 Cut the tops off the aubergines and discard them. Carefully scoop out the flesh without breaking the skin, leaving a 5 mm (¼ in) thickness of flesh all round. Be careful not to cut through the end. Rinse and drain.

2 Prepare the stuffing by combining all the stuffing ingredients in a large bowl. Fill the aubergine hollows to three-quarters full with the stuffing, leaving enough space at the top for the rice to expand. Sprinkle the top of the aubergines with salt.

3 Arrange the aubergines horizontally in a large saucepan, cover with the water, then press with a slightly smaller saucepan lid that fits inside the saucepan. Then cover with the pan's lid and bring to the boil over a high heat. Reduce the heat and cook gently for approximately 45 minutes, until the aubergines are almost tender.

4 Dissolve the tomato paste in 250 ml (9 fl oz) water and add to the saucepan. Bring to the boil again until the aubergines are tender. Remove from the heat and set aside to cool. Serve cold.

Bulgur pilaf

Bulgur pilavi

SERVES 8
COOKING TIME: 30 MINUTES

500 g (1 lb 2 oz) coarse bulgur
100 g (3½ oz) butter
2 medium onions, peeled and finely chopped
3 large tomatoes, peeled, de-seeded and diced
2 small sweet green peppers, de-seeded
  and finely chopped
1 tsp salt
Pinch of freshly ground black pepper
600 ml (1 pint) meat stock

1 Rinse the bulgur in plenty of water and drain.

2 Melt the butter in a saucepan, fry the onions until soft, then add the bulgur and stir over a medium heat for about 5 minutes. Add the tomatoes, peppers, salt and pepper, and stir well. Remove from the heat.

3 In a separate pan, bring the meat stock to the boil, then add it to the bulgur mixture. Stir and cover, bring to the boil, then cook on a low heat until the liquid has evaporated.

4 Remove from the heat, cover with a dry kitchen cloth and replace the lid. Allow to stand for 10 minutes, stir thoroughly and let stand for another 5 minutes. Pour into a serving dish and serve cold.

Stuffed vine leaves

Dolmades

SERVES 6
COOKING TIME: 1 HOUR

400 g (14 oz) fresh vine leaves
Juice of 1 lemon

For the filling
3 artichoke hearts, grated
2 potatoes, peeled and grated
3 courgettes, grated
3 onions, peeled and grated
500 g (1 lb 2 oz) white rice
Small bunch of parsley, finely chopped
Small bunch of fresh mint, finely chopped
230 ml (8 fl oz) olive oil
1 tsp salt
1 tsp freshly ground black pepper

1 Blanch the vine leaves in a bowl of hot water for 5 minutes, then remove from the heat, strain and separate them.

2 In a separate bowl, mix together the filling ingredients.

3 Place a teaspoon of the filling into the centre of each vine leaf, then fold the leaf over to make a parcel. Repeat with all the mixture and vine leaves.

4 Place the vine leaf parcels in a pan, cover with hot water, then cover and simmer gently for approximately 1 hour.

5 Once cooked, remove the dolmades from the pan with a slotted spoon, arrange on a serving dish and pour the lemon juice over them. Serve cold.

Pilaf with aubergines

Zeytinyagli patlicanli pilav

SERVES 10
COOKING TIME: 30 MINUTES

8 long, thin aubergines
700 g (1 lb 9 oz) arborio rice
2 tsp salt
2 tsp caster sugar
2 Tbsp sunflower oil
950 ml (33 fl oz) olive oil
7 medium onions, peeled and finely chopped
5 mild green chillies, finely chopped
2 tomatoes peeled, de-seeded and diced
950 ml (33 fl oz) water
1 tsp allspice
Sprig of dill, finely chopped
Sprig of fresh mint, finely chopped

1 Rinse and partially peel the aubergines in alternate lengthways strips. Remove and discard the stalks and cut the aubergines into small cubes. Soak in salted water for about 20 minutes to remove any bitter juices.

2 Place the rice in a bowl, cover with hot water and stir in 1 tablespoon of salt. Let stand for 10 minutes, then rinse thoroughly and drain.

3 Remove the aubergines from the water, squeeze gently and pat dry with kitchen paper. Sprinkle 1 teaspoon of salt and sugar over the aubergine cubes and rub in well. Fry the cubes in the sunflower oil until golden brown, then drain on kitchen paper.

4 Heat the olive oil in a pan and fry the onions, chillies and tomatoes until lightly cooked, then stir in the water and the remaining teaspoons of salt and sugar and the allspice. Bring to the boil and stir in the rice. Cover and bring to the boil, then lower the heat and cook gently until the rice has absorbed the liquid.

5 Sprinkle the dill and mint over the rice and lay the aubergines over the top. Cover and cook for 5 minutes on a low heat, then remove from the heat and stand for 20 minutes. Stir the rice, cover and stand for a further 2 minutes. Transfer to a serving dish and serve cold.

Dried beans with tomato and spinach

Fasolia xera yachnista

SERVES 6
COOKING TIME: 1 HOUR 15 MINUTES

500 g (1 lb 2 oz) dried mixed beans (to include
   broad, kidney and pinto beans)
120 ml (4 fl oz) olive oil
1 onion, peeled and finely chopped
Small bunch of dill, finely chopped
500 g (1 lb 2 oz) tomatoes, finely chopped
1 tsp salt
1 tsp freshly ground black pepper
650 ml (23 fl oz) water
1 kg (2 lb 3 oz) spinach, finely chopped

1   Place the beans in a large pot and cover well with salted water. Boil for 30 minutes, then drain.

2   Heat the olive oil in a pan and fry the onion and dill for 10 minutes.

3   Add the beans and tomatoes to the pan, along with the salt, pepper and water. Simmer for 10 minutes until almost cooked. Add the spinach and simmer for a further 15 minutes. Remove from the heat, allow to cool and serve cold.

LEBANON

Potatoes in oil and lemon dressing

Batata bil zeit wal hamoud

SERVES 4
COOKING TIME: 25 MINUTES

1 kg (2 lb 3 oz) new potatoes, unpeeled
2 garlic cloves, peeled and crushed
50 ml (1¾ fl oz) lemon juice
100 ml (3½ fl oz) olive oil
Pinch of salt and white pepper
100 g (3½ oz) fresh parsley, chopped, to garnish

1   Rinse the potatoes and boil whole in a saucepan of boiling, salted water until cooked. Remove from the heat, drain and leave to cool. Peel the potatoes and cut into medium cubes, then transfer to a serving dish.

2   In a bowl, mix the garlic with the lemon juice and olive oil. Season with salt and white pepper. Add the sauce to the potato cubes and mix well. Sprinkle with parsley and serve cold.

Fish filet in tahini sauce

Tajin el samak

SERVES 6
COOKING TIME: 30 MINUTES

1 kg (2 lb 3 oz) sea bass filets, sliced
50 ml (1¾ fl oz) olive oil
2 onions, peeled and sliced
200 g (7 oz) tahini
200 ml (7 fl oz) water
100 ml (3½ fl oz) lemon juice
1 tsp salt
Pinch of white pepper
1 tsp cumin
½ tsp Tabasco sauce
50 g (2 oz) walnuts, crushed
50 g (2 oz) pine nuts, toasted
Vegetable oil, for frying
4 pitta pockets
1 lemon, cut into wedges, to garnish
Fresh parsley leaves, to garnish

1 Arrange the fish filets in an oven tray. Bake for 15 minutes then leave to cool.

2 Heat the olive oil in a small pan and fry the onions until golden brown. Add in the tahini, water, lemon juice, salt, pepper, cumin, Tabasco and walnuts. Cook the mixture until it thickens to a paste-like consistency. Pour over the fish filets and sprinkle with pine nuts.

3 Fry the bread in the vegetable oil. Drain over absorbent paper, then arrange around a serving platter with the fish in the centre. Garnish with the lemon wedges and parsley.

Broad beans in lemon, olive oil and garlic

Fasulye aridah moutabaleh

SERVES 5
COOKING TIME: 1 HOUR 15 MINUTES

350 g (12½ oz) broad beans, soaked in water
   for 10 hours or overnight
75 ml (2½ fl oz) olive oil

For the dressing
3 garlic cloves, peeled and crushed
50 ml (1¾ fl oz) lemon juice
Pinch of salt

1 Rinse the pre-soaked broad beans, drain and transfer to a pan. Cover with cold water and cook over a high heat for about 1 hour, until tender. Transfer to a serving dish and allow to cool.

2 To prepare the dressing, mix the garlic with the lemon juice and salt. Pour over the broad beans and drizzle the olive oil on top.

TURKEY

Beetroot dip

Yogurtlu pancar mezesi

SERVES 8–10

3 beetroots
Juice of ½ lemon
1 garlic clove, peeled and crushed
5 Tbsp Greek yoghurt
Pinch of salt
1 Tbsp olive oil
Pitta bread, to serve

1 Boil the beetroots for approximately 15 minutes, or until cooked, or microwave with 2 tablespoons of water for 4 minutes.

2 Place the beetroots, lemon juice and garlic in a blender and blend together until smooth. Add the yoghurt and salt, and blend again until smooth.

3 Transfer to a serving dish, drizzle with the olive oil and serve with hot pitta breads.

Vine leaves with rice stuffing

Zeytinyagli yaprak dolmasi

SERVES 10
COOKING TIME: 1 HOUR 40 MINUTES

For the stuffing
130 g (4½ oz) white rice
2 Tbsp currants
100 ml (3½ fl oz) olive oil
100 ml (3½ fl oz) sunflower oil
2 Tbsp pine kernels
6 medium onions, peeled and finely chopped
1 tsp cinnamon
1 tsp allspice
1 tsp white pepper
1 tsp salt
100 ml (3½ fl oz) hot water
½ bunch of fresh mint, chopped
Bunch of dill, chopped

400 g (14 oz) fresh vine leaves
100 ml (3½ fl oz) olive oil
1 tsp caster sugar
2.4 litres (4¼ pints) cold water
1 lemon, peeled and sliced

1 Prepare the stuffing by soaking the rice in cold water for 30 minutes, then rinsing thoroughly and draining. Soak the currants in warm water for about 15 minutes until they swell.

2 In a frying pan, heat the olive and sunflower oils, then add the pine kernels and onions and brown slightly. Add the soaked rice and cook for 10 minutes. Then add the soaked currants, spices, salt and hot water, and cook over a low heat for 15 minutes, until the water has evaporated. Remove from the heat, then stir in the mint and dill and set aside to cool.

3 Scald the vine leaves in boiling water, then dip in cold water to preserve their colour. If the leaves are preserved in brine, soak them in warm water and rinse thoroughly to remove the excess salt.

4 Open each leaf with the glossy side facing down and veins facing upwards. Place a teaspoon of the rice filling at the base of each leaf and fold the edges inwards over the stuffing, then roll up to form a finger-sized dolma. Repeat until all the mixture is finished. There should be about 30 dolmas in total. Place any discarded coarse leaves at the bottom of a saucepan. Layer the stuffed vine leaves over them with the folded edges facing down.

5 In a small bowl, mix the olive oil and sugar together and pour over the vine leaves. Pour over the water. Arrange the lemon slices on top and a damp sheet of greaseproof paper over this, weighted down with a plate. Cover and bring to the boil over a high heat, then simmer for approximately 45 minutes. When most of the water has evaporated and the vine leaves are tender, set aside to cool with the lid on.

Green beans

Zeytinyag̃   sulye

SERVES 10
COOKING TIME: 1 HOUR

1.5 kg (3 lb 5 oz) runner beans or French beans
2 medium tomatoes
120 ml (4 fl oz) olive oil
½ tsp tomato paste
2 large onions, peeled
1 tsp salt
3 tsp caster sugar
950 ml (33 fl oz) water

1 Rinse the beans, then top and tail them.

2 Peel, de-seed and dice the tomatoes, then lightly fry in the olive oil with the tomato paste until it forms a purée.

3 Arrange the beans in neat layers in a broad pan. Place the whole peeled onions on top. Strain the tomato purée and pour over.

4 Add the salt, sugar and water, and cover with a circle of damp greaseproof paper weighted down with a plate. Bring to the boil on a high heat, then cook over a low heat for approximately 1 hour, or until most of the liquid has evaporated and the beans are tender. Set aside to cool.

5 Drain the liquid into a bowl, remove and discard the onions and turn the beans upside down into a serving dish. Pour the liquid over and serve cold.

Mixed bean salad

Palikaria

SERVES 4
COOKING TIME: 45 MINUTES

100 g (3½ oz) dried mixed beans
   (to include kidney, pinto and broad beans)
100 g (3½ oz) millet
100 g (3½ oz) burghul (cracked wheat)
100 g (3½ oz) dried chickpeas
100 g (3½ oz) dried lentils
100 g (3½ oz) frozen peas
1 tsp salt
1 tsp freshly ground black pepper
2 spring onions, finely chopped
1 Tbsp dill, finely chopped
120 ml (4 fl oz) olive oil
2 Tbsp lemon juice

1 Soak all the pulses, except for the lentils and peas, in water overnight. Soak the burghul and chickpeas separately to allow for more time cooking.

2 The following day, drain the burghul and chickpeas and place in a pan with plenty of water and boil for 30 minutes.

3 Then add the remaining soaked and drained pulses, along with the lentils and peas, and boil for about 15 minutes until they are soft. Drain and place in a serving bowl, and season with salt and pepper.

4 In a bowl, mix together the spring onions, dill, olive oil and lemon juice, then drizzle over the salad. Serve cold.

GREECE

Fish roe dip

Taramosalata

SERVES 4
COOKING TIME: 30 MINUTES

1 large potato, peeled and cut into 1 cm (⅜ in) cubes
115 g (4 oz) codfish roe
½ onion, peeled and minced
3 Tbsp fresh lemon juice
115 ml (4 fl oz) olive oil
1 black olive, to garnish
Warm pitta bread, to serve

1 Place the potato cubes in a saucepan and cover with water. Bring to the boil, then reduce the heat and simmer until cooked through. Drain and set aside to cool.

2 Transfer the potato pieces to a bowl, along with the roe, onion and lemon juice, and blend until smooth.

3 Add the olive oil and blend to a smooth, creamy consistency. Transfer to a serving bowl, garnish with the olive and refrigerate until cold. Serve with warm pitta bread.

Hot chilli tahini dip

Tarator har

SERVES 4

1 garlic clove, peeled
Pinch salt
Juice of 1 lemon
20 g (¾ oz) tahini
50 ml (1¾ fl oz) water
Pinch of hot paprika
1 green chilli, de-seeded and chopped
Warm bread, to serve

1 In a bowl, crush the garlic with the salt. Mix in the lemon juice and tahini.

2 Gradually mix in the water until the dip is smooth. Stir in the hot paprika and chopped pepper. Transfer to a serving dish. Serve with warm bread.

Swooning imam

Imam bayildi

SERVES 10
COOKING TIME: 1 HOUR 30 MINUTES

10 medium aubergines
Sunflower oil, for frying
200 ml (7 fl oz) olive oil
6 medium onions, peeled and finely chopped
6 large tomatoes peeled, de-seeded and diced
6 garlic cloves, peeled and crushed
Bunch of parsley, chopped
1 tsp salt
1 Tbsp caster sugar
400 ml (14 fl oz) water
Juice of 1 lemon

1 Rinse the aubergines, remove the stalks and partially peel the aubergines in alternate strips. Fry the aubergines whole in sunflower oil until golden brown, then split open lengthways leaving both ends uncut.

2 Place the aubergines in a shallow saucepan side by side in a single layer with the open sides facing upwards and set aside.

3 Heat half the olive oil in a pan and fry the onions until lightly browned. Add the tomatoes, garlic, parsley and salt and simmer for 15 minutes. Remove the mixture from the heat and stuff the aubergines with it.

4 In a bowl, mix together the sugar, water, lemon juice and the remaining olive oil and pour over the aubergines. Cover and cook on a medium heat for 1 hour or until tender. Transfer to a serving platter and serve cold.

Stuffed cabbage leaves

Lahanodolmades

SERVES 6
COOKING TIME: 1 HOUR 30 MINUTES

1 large cabbage, rinsed and separated into leaves
2 Tbsp olive oil

For the filling
Small fennel bulb, finely chopped
Small bunch of parsley, finely chopped
Small bunch of fresh mint, finely chopped
4 tomatoes, grated
3 onions, peeled and grated
500 g (1 lb 2 oz) white rice
1 tsp salt
1 tsp freshly ground black pepper

1 Blanch the cabbage leaves in a bowl of hot water for 5 minutes, then remove from the water and separate them. In a large bowl mix together the filling ingredients.

2 Place a teaspoon of the filling into the centre of each cabbage leaf, then fold the leaf over to make a parcel. Repeat until all the mixture is finished and you have filled approximately 30 dolmades, making sure you set aside about four cabbage leaves. Shred these leaves.

3 Pour the olive oil in a saucepan, then layer the shredded cabbage leaves on the bottom of the pan. Place the dolmades in circles on top of the shredded leaves.

4 Add water to cover the parcels and 2 tablespoons of olive oil and simmer until the water is absorbed. While cooking, occasionally gently shake the pot to stop the lower cabbage leaves from sticking to the bottom of the pan. When cooked, remove from the pan, allow to cool and serve cold.

Aubergines with tomatoes

Batinjan bil banadoora

SERVES 6
COOKING TIME: 1 HOUR 15 MINUTES

6 long, thin aubergines
150 ml (5 fl oz) olive oil
Juice of ½ lemon
200 ml (7 fl oz) water

For the stuffing
3 medium onions, peeled and finely chopped
3 large peeled tomatoes, de-seeded and chopped
1 Tbsp salt
1 Tbsp caster sugar
1 large garlic clove, peeled and crushed
½ bunch of parsley, chopped

1 Start by preparing the aubergines. Cut off the tops and partially peel the aubergines in alternate strips. Make a deep lengthways score down each aubergine without cutting right to either end. Mix one tablespoon of salt into a large bowl of water and soak the aubergines for 30 minutes.

2 Prepare the stuffing by combining all the stuffing ingredients together. Drain and rinse the aubergines, dry well and arrange in a shallow saucepan. Fill the splits of aubergines with the stuffing.

3 Pour the olive oil, lemon juice and water over the aubergines, then press with a slightly smaller saucepan lid that fits inside the saucepan. Then cover with the pan's lid and bring to the boil over a high heat. Reduce the heat and cook gently for approximately 45 minutes, until the aubergines are tender and the liquid has evaporated.

4 Set aside to cool with the saucepan lid on. Carefully transfer the aubergines to a serving dish and serve cold.

TURKEY

Artichokes with broad beans

Zeytinyagli ic baklali enginar

SERVES 10
COOKING TIME: 1 HOUR

10 artichoke hearts
Juice of 2 lemons
2 tsp salt
7 tsp plain flour
3 medium onions, peeled and chopped
1.8 litres (3 pints) water
6 tsp caster sugar
120 ml (4 fl oz) olive oil

For the broad beans
850 g (1 lb 14 oz) broad beans
3 large onions, peeled and chopped
950 ml (33 fl oz) water
400 ml (14 fl oz) olive oil
5 tsp sugar
2 tsp salt
3 sprigs of dill, chopped, to garnish

1 Rub the artichoke hearts with the juice of one of the lemons and salt to avoid discoloration, then place the hearts in a pan along with the juice from the remaining lemon, flour, onions, water, sugar and olive oil.

2 Cover with a sheet of greaseproof paper pushed down into the saucepan and weighted down with a plate. Cook over a gentle heat for 45 minutes.

3 In the meantime prepare the broad beans. Shell them, remove the skin and place in a pan with the onions, water, olive oil, sugar and salt. Cook over a medium heat for approximately 1 hour, or until beans are tender. Remove from the heat and allow to cool.

4 Remove the artichokes from the heat and set aside to cool without removing the cover. When cooled, place the artichokes on a serving dish and fill the centres with the broad bean mixture. Cover with the juice from the cooked artichokes and garnish with dill.

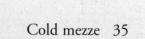

Yoghurt dip
Tzatziki

SERVES 4

530 ml (19 fl oz) strained yoghurt
1 cucumber, peeled and finely diced
4 garlic cloves, peeled and crushed
1 Tbsp olive oil
Pinch of salt and freshly ground black pepper
Warm pitta bread, to serve

1 Blend the yoghurt, cucumber and g_____ssor until smooth.

2 Add the olive oil, salt and pepper, and blend again. Pour into a serving bowl and refrigerate until chilled. Serve with warm pitta bread.

LEBANON

Fried aubergines with yoghurt dip
Batinjan makli ma salsat el laban

SERVES 4
COOKING TIME: 15 MINUTES

2 large aubergines
Salt and white pepper
800 ml (28 fl oz) vegetable oil

For the dip
Pinch of salt
1 garlic clove, peeled
400 ml (14 fl oz) plain yoghurt
3 medium cucumbers, cubed
1 Tbsp dried mint

1 Remove the tops of the aubergines and cut into thick rounds. Season with salt and pepper and leave to drain on absorbent paper.

2 To prepare the dip crush the salt with the garlic in a bowl. Stir in the yoghurt, then mix in the cucumber and mint. Refrigerate until chilled.

3 In the meantime, fry the aubergine rounds in the oil until golden brown. Drain on absorbent paper and serve with the yoghurt dip on the side.

Walnut dip

Mohamra

SERVES 8–10

3 garlic cloves, peeled
3 jalapeño peppers, chopped
175 g (6 oz) chopped walnuts
1 medium red pepper, de-seeded and chopped
1 small onion, peeled and finely chopped
2 Tbsp molasses
2 Tbsp olive oil
1 Tbsp ground cumin
Pinch of salt
Hot pitta bread, to serve

Blend all the ingredient̶ ̶m̶i̶x̶t̶u̶r̶e̶ forms a smooth consistency. Place in a serving dish and serve with hot pitta bread.

LEBANON

Swiss chard in tahini dip

Silq bil tahini

SERVES 5
COOKING TIME: 30 MINUTES

1 kg (1 lb 2 oz) Swiss chard, leaves discarded
1 garlic clove, peeled and crushed
Pinch of salt
200 g (7 oz) tahini
75 ml (2½ fl oz) lemon juice
2 Tbsp fresh chopped parsley, to garnish

1 Rinse the Swiss chard stalks and remove any thin fine veins using a sharp kitchen knife. Cut the stalks into 3 cm (1¼ in) pieces, then transfer to a saucepan and cover with water. Cook over a medium heat until tender. Remove from heat and leave to cool. Drain and transfer to a large salad bowl.

2 In a small bowl, mix the garlic with the salt, tahini, lemon juice and a little water until smooth. Add the mix to Swiss chard stalks and mix well. Sprinkle fresh parsley on top to garnish and serve cold.

Aubergines with rice stuffing

Zeytinyagli patlican ⬚

SERVES 10
COOKING TIME: 1 HOUR 40 MINUTES

For the stuffing
130 g (4½ oz) white rice
2 Tbsp currants
100 ml (3½ fl oz) olive oil
100 ml (3½ fl oz) sunflower oil
2 Tbsp pine kernels
6 medium onions, peeled and finely chopped
1 tsp cinnamon
1 tsp allspice
1 tsp white pepper
1 tsp caster sugar
1 tsp salt
100 ml (3½ fl oz) hot water
½ bunch of fresh mint, chopped
Bunch of dill, chopped

10 medium aubergines
Juice of 1 lemon
100 ml (3½ fl oz) olive oil
Pinch of salt and sugar
400 ml (14 fl oz) hot water

1   Start by preparing the stuffing. Soak the rice in cold water for 30 minutes, then rinse thoroughly and drain. Soak the currants in a little warm water for about 15 minutes until they swell, then drain. In a frying pan, heat the olive and sunflower oils and fry the pine kernels and onions until lightly browned. Add the rice and cook for 10 minutes. Add the soaked currants, spices, sugar, salt and hot water, and cook over a low heat for 15 minutes until the water has evaporated. Stir in the mint and dill. Set aside to cool.

2   De-stalk and hollow out the aubergines. Keep the cores to one side and cut into 1 cm (3/8 in) lengths. Place the cored aubergines in a large bowl of water with the lemon juice to prevent discoloration.

3   Preheat the oven to 190° C (375° F/gas 5). Fill the aubergines with the rice stuffing and plug with the cores fixed in place with cocktail sticks.

4   Prick the skin of the stuffed aubergines in several places and place in a deep baking tray. In a bowl, mix together the olive oil, salt and sugar, and pour over aubergines. Pour over the hot water. Place a damp sheet of greaseproof paper over the aubergines with ends tucked in. Bake for approximately 25 minutes, then set aside to cool.

Beirut-style chickpea dip

Hommus beiruty

SERVES 4
COOKING TIME: 15 MINUTES

420 g (15 oz) tinned, cooked chickpeas
2 garlic cloves, peeled and crushed
180 ml (6 fl oz) water
4 Tbsp tahini
125 ml (4 fl oz) lemon juice
3 Tbsp fresh parsley, chopped
Pinch of salt
2 Tbsp olive oil
3 Tbsp tinned, cooked broad beans

1 In a food processor, blend the chickpeas with the garlic and half the water until smooth.

2 Dissolve the tahini in the lemon juice and remaining water, then blend with the chickpea mixture. The mixture should be thick and smooth. Mix in the fresh parsley and season with salt.

3 Transfer the mixture to small serving dishes and garnish with the olive oil and cooked broad beans.

 TURKEY

Broad bean purée

Fava

SERVES 10
COOKING TIME: 30 MINUTES

500 g (1 lb 2 oz) dried broad beans
350 g (12½ oz) fresh broad beans, shelled
950 ml (33 fl oz) water
1 large onion, peeled and chopped
3 small potatoes, peeled and diced
200 ml (7 fl oz) olive oil
2 Tbsp sunflower oil
2 tsp salt
4 tsp caster sugar
1 Tbsp fresh dill, chopped

1 Rinse the dried beans, place them in a saucepan with the fresh shelled beans and the water. Add the onion, potatoes, olive and sunflower oils, salt and sugar, and cook over a medium heat until the ingredients form a purée.

2 Use an electric blender or press the mixture through a wire strainer to form a smooth, thick purée. Pour into a bowl and leave to cool.

3 If not serving immediately, cover with cling film or a damp cloth and place in the refrigerator. When ready to serve, transfer to a serving dish and garnish with the dill.   .

Circassian chicken

Cerkez tavugu

SERVES 10
COOKING TIME: 45 MINUTES

1 large chicken
850 ml (1½ pints) water
1 medium potato, peeled and chopped
1 small onion, peeled and chopped
1 carrot, peeled and chopped
½ tsp salt

For the walnut sauce
400 g (14 oz) shelled walnuts
2 slices stale white bread, crusts removed
2 tsp ground red peppercorns
2 garlic cloves, peeled and crushed
½ tsp salt

1 Rinse the chicken and place it in a large pan with the water. Add the potato, onion and carrot, and bring to the boil. When the chicken is part cooked add the salt, cover and continue to boil until the chicken is tender.

2 Remove the chicken, strain off the stock into a separate bowl, separate the bones and skin, and cut the meat into small pieces.

3 To make the sauce, crush the walnuts or pound to a paste in a pestle and mortar, then place in a mixing bowl.

4 Soak the bread in the chicken stock, squeeze out the moisture and crumble into the walnuts, then mix until smooth. Add the peppercorns, garlic and salt and knead together. Place the mixture in a piece of muslin and squeeze the moisture out into a bowl.

5 Transfer the muslin mixture to a bowl, then beat in 250 ml (9 fl oz) of the warm chicken stock until a pouring consistency is achieved.

6 Place the chicken pieces into a serving bowl and pour over the walnut sauce.

Mackerel salad

Uskumru salatasi

SERVES 2
COOKING TIME: 10 MINUTES

For the salad
½ crisphead lettuce
Handful of fresh rocket leaves
6 sprigs of dill, chopped
2 mackerel
350 ml (12 fl oz) sunflower oil
1 Tbsp olive oil for frying
1 tsp pine nuts
1 large tomato, peeled, de-seeded and sliced
1 Tbsp currants, soaked

For the dressing
125 ml (4 fl oz) olive oil
Juice of ½ lemon
½ tsp mustard
1 tsp white wine vinegar
1 Tbsp chicken stock
Pinch of salt and freshly ground black pepper

1 Start by preparing the salad. Rinse the lettuce and rocket and shred. Rinse the dill and remove the stalks.

2 Gut the mackerel, remove the gills and rinse thoroughly. Pat dry. Fry the mackerel in the sunflower oil and allow to cool before flaking.

3 Heat the olive oil in a pan and fry the pine nuts until golden brown.

4 Arrange the lettuce and rocket in a dome in the centre of a serving bowl. Place the slices of fish and tomato around the centre. Sprinkle the pine nuts, currants and chopped dill over the fish.

5 Prepare the dressing by mixing together the olive oil, lemon juice, mustard, vinegar, stock, salt and pepper, then drizzle over the salad.

Lentil burghul

Moudardara

SERVES 5
COOKING TIME: 1 HOUR

350 g (12½ oz) lentils
1 litre (1¾ pints) water
150 g (5½ oz) burghul (cracked wheat)
Pinch of salt and white pepper
100 ml (3½ fl oz) olive oil
3 onions, peeled and sliced

1 Rinse the lentils and place them in a saucepan with the water. Bring to the boil, then reduce the heat. Cover and simmer for 30 minutes until the lentils are almost tender.

2 Rinse the burghul and add it to the saucepan. Season with salt. Simmer over a low heat for about 15 minutes.

3 In the meantime, heat the olive oil in a pan and fry the onions over a moderate heat until golden brown. Reserve one third of the quantity for garnishing. Add the remaining onions with their oil to the lentils saucepan. Season with white pepper and simmer for 10 minutes until the liquid is absorbed and the burghul and lentils are tender. Pour in a serving dish and garnish with the reserved browned onions.

Hot mezze

Sultan's delight

Hunkar begendi

SERVES 6
COOKING TIME: 1 HOUR 30 MINUTES

3 Tbsp butter
2 medium onions, peeled and finely chopped
1 kg (2 lb 3 oz) leg of lamb, cubed
2 garlic cloves, peeled and crushed
2 large tomatoes, peeled, de-seeded and diced
1 small sweet green pepper, de-seeded and
   finely chopped
300 ml (½ pint) hot water
1 tsp salt
1 tsp peppercorns

For the aubergine purée
1.5 kg (3 lb 5 oz) aubergines
125 g (4½ oz) butter
3 Tbsp plain flour
400 ml (14 fl oz) warm milk
Pinch of salt
4 Tbsp grated mature kasar or cheddar cheese
Pinch of grated nutmeg

1 Heat the butter in a pan and fry the onions until softened, then add the lamb and cook over a medium heat, stirring occasionally, for 10 minutes. Add the garlic, tomatoes and pepper, and cook until the juice has evaporated.

2 Stir in the hot water, salt and peppercorns, cover and bring to the boil. Lower the heat and cook over a medium heat for approximately 1 hour.

3 To prepare the aubergine purée, rinse the aubergines and pierce the skin in several places with cocktail sticks and cook over an open gas flame or charcoal fire, turning occasionally until the skin is charred and the flesh is tender.

4 In the meantime, melt the butter in a large saucepan, sprinkle over the flour and stir, then remove from the heat.

5 Holding the aubergines by their stalks, scrape away the skin, then remove the stalks and add to the saucepan. Mash the aubergines and place the saucepan over a medium heat, blending together, and gradually adding in the warm milk and salt.

6 When the mixture bubbles, remove it from the heat, add the cheese and nutmeg, and stir well. Pour the aubergine purée into a serving bowl, hollow out the centre and arrange the meat in its juices into the centre. Serve hot.

Split pea croquettes

Fava keftedes

SERVES 4–6
COOKING TIME: 1 HOUR

500 g (1 lb 2 oz) yellow split peas
1 onion, peeled and grated
Small bunch of parsley, finely chopped
170 g (6 oz) breadcrumbs
170 g (6 oz) feta cheese, crumbled
2 medium eggs, beaten
Pinch of salt and freshly ground black pepper
Plain flour, for coating the croquettes
Olive oil, for frying

1 Rinse the peas in a sieve under running water, then place in a large saucepan. Add water and bring to the boil.

2 Once boiled, add the onion and simmer over a low heat for 50 minutes, until thick. Remove from the heat and set aside to cool.

3 Add the parsley, breadcrumbs, cheese, eggs, salt and pepper, and mix together to form a thick consistency.

4 Knead the mixture and shape into golf ball-sized balls. Coat each ball in flour and fry in olive oil until golden.

 LEBANON

Fried eggs with minced meat

Bayd bi kawarma

SERVES 4
COOKING TIME: 5 MINUTES

100 ml (3½ fl oz) olive oil
200 g (7 oz) lean lamb, minced
6 medium eggs
Pinch white pepper

1 Heat the olive oil in a pan and fry the minced meat until brown and tender.

2 Break the eggs over the meat and season with white pepper. Mix well and cook until the egg whites run dry. Transfer to a serving dish and serve immediately.

Broad beans and artichokes

Koukia me aginares

SERVES 4–6
COOKING TIME: 45 MINUTES

8 artichoke hearts, halved
2 Tbsp lemon juice
1 kg (2 lb 3 oz) fresh broad beans
125 ml (4½ fl oz) olive oil
Small bunch of dill, finely chopped
2 fresh garlic leaves, chopped
Pinch of salt and freshly ground black pepper
2 Tbsp plain flour
2 Tbsp white wine vinegar

1 Rub the artichoke hearts with the lemon juice and set aside. Top and tail the broad beans.

2 Heat the oil in a saucepan and sauté the dill and garlic leaves for a couple of minutes.

3 Add the beans and cover with 250 ml (9 fl oz) water. Simmer for 15 minutes. Add the artichokes, salt and pepper. Stir well and simmer for about 20 minutes, or until the artichokes are almost tender.

4 In a bowl, dilute the flour in 100 ml (3½ fl oz) water, then add the vinegar. Remove 3 to 4 tablespoons of liquid from the pan and stir into the flour mixture. Pour this mixture back into the pan, stir well and cook for 5 minutes. Serve hot.

Rabbit in wine and garlic sauce

Kouneli me aspri saltsa

SERVES 4
COOKING TIME: 1 HOUR

Small rabbit, skinned, gutted and cut into
    small portions
200 ml (7 fl oz) white wine
125 ml (4 fl oz) olive oil
5 garlic cloves, peeled and crushed
Pinch of salt and freshly ground black pepper
50 g (2 oz) plain flour
2 sprigs of rosemary, chopped
Juice of 1 lemon

1 Place the rabbit pieces in a bowl with half the wine and marinate for 30 minutes.

2 Place the rabbit pieces in a pan with the oil, garlic, salt and pepper, and lightly brown. Add the flour, rosemary, lemon juice and remaining wine, and simmer for approximately 30 minutes or until the meat is tender and cooked.

Spinach pies
Spanakopita

SERVES 6
COOKING TIME: 40 MINUTES

125 ml (4 fl oz) olive oil
1 onion, peeled and finely chopped
3 spring onions, finely chopped
2 garlic cloves, peeled and minced
1 kg (2 lb 3 oz) spinach leaves, rinsed
   and finely chopped
Small bunch of parsley, finely chopped
Small bunch of mint, finely chopped
2 medium eggs, lightly beaten
115 g (4 oz) feta cheese, crumbled
100 g (3½ oz) ricotta cheese
8 sheets filo pastry
2 Tbsp butter, for greasing

1 Preheat the oven to 190º C (375º F/gas 5) and grease a
25 cm (10 in) square baking pan with butter.

2 Heat the olive oil in a pan and fry the onion, spring onions
and garlic until lightly browned. Add in the spinach, parsley
and mint, and sauté briefly until the spinach is wilted.
Remove from the heat and set aside to cool.

3 In a bowl, mix together the eggs, feta and ricotta cheeses,
then stir into the spinach mixture and combine thoroughly.

4 Lay a sheet of filo pastry in the baking pan and lightly
brush with olive oil. Then layer three more sheets of filo
overlapping the first, each brushed with oil.

5 Spread the spinach and cheese mixture over the pastry and
fold the overhanging pastry over the filling and brush with oil.

6 Layer the remaining four sheets of filo, each brushed with
oil, over the mixture. Tuck the pastry around to seal the
filling. Bake for 30 minutes or until golden. Once cooked,
cut into squares and serve hot.

Fried fish with tahini sauce

Samak makli ma el tarator

SERVES 4
COOKING TIME: 20 MINUTES

2 kg (4 lb 6 oz) red mullet
Plain flour, for coating the fish
1 litre (35 fl oz) vegetable oil
6 pitta pockets
2 lemons, cut into wedges, to garnish

For the stuffing
1 Tbsp butter
Bunch of coriander, finely chopped
1 garlic clove, peeled and crushed
Pinch of salt and white pepper

For the sauce
50 g (2 oz) tahini
50 ml (1¾ fl oz) lemon juice
50 ml (1¾ fl oz) water
1 garlic clove, peeled and crushed
Salt and freshly ground black pepper

1 Clean and scale the fish. Rinse thoroughly and drain.

2 Prepare the stuffing by combining all the ingredients together and stuffing the fish with the mixture. Seal the fish at the sides with toothpicks.

3 Coat the fish with flour. Heat the vegetable oil in a frying pan and fry the fish over a high heat for 5 to 7 minutes on each side, until tender and golden brown.

4 In the meantime combine all the sauce ingredients together and mix well until smooth.

5 Carefully lift the fish out of the pan and drain on absorbent paper. Fry the pitta bread in the same oil until golden brown. Arrange the fish on a serving dish and garnish with lemon wedges. Serve hot along with the toasted fried bread and tahini sauce.

Aubergines with yoghurt sauce

Fattet el batinjan

SERVES 4
COOKING TIME: 50 MINUTES

400 g (14 oz) lean lamb, from the leg
100 g (3½ oz) leeks, cut into chunks
30 g (1 oz) fresh dill, chopped
2 bay leaves
2 cloves
1 kg (2 lb 3 oz) aubergines, cubed and soaked
   for 6 hours in salted water
50 g (2 oz) plain flour
200 ml (7 fl oz) vegetable oil, for frying
Pinch of salt and white pepper
4 garlic cloves, peeled and crushed
800 ml (28 fl oz) plain yoghurt
4 pitta pockets, cut into pieces
50 g (2 oz) pine nuts
Pinch of dried mint

1 Trim away any excess fat from the meat and cut into 2.5 cm (1 in) cubes. Transfer to a large saucepan and cover with water. Bring to the boil until the fat floats to the surface, then remove it with a large spoon. Add in the leeks, dill, bay leaves and cloves. Cook the meat for about 20 minutes, or until tender.

2 In the meantime, rinse the aubergine cubes, drain and toss in the flour. Heat half the vegetable oil in a pan and fry the aubergine cubes until brown. Drain on absorbent paper, then add to the meat. Season the mixture with salt and pepper and bring to the boil, then reduce the heat and simmer for 10 minutes.

3 In a small saucepan mix the garlic with the yoghurt and season with salt. Bring to the boil, stirring constantly, then remove from the heat and set aside.

4 Fry the bread in the remaining vegetable oil until golden brown, then drain on absorbent paper. Fry the pine nuts until brown, then drain and set aside.

5 Arrange the bread in a serving platter. Cover with the aubergine and meat cubes. Top with the yoghurt and pine nuts and sprinkle with mint. Serve immediately.

Islim kebab with aubergines

Patlicanli islim kebabi

SERVES 6
COOKING TIME: 1 HOUR 30 MINUTES

3 Tbsp butter
750 g (1 lb 10 oz) cubed lamb
2 medium onions, peeled and finely chopped
2 garlic cloves, peeled and crushed
3 large tomatoes, peeled, de-seeded and diced
2 mild green chillies, de-seeded and finely chopped
950 ml (33 fl oz) hot water
1 tsp salt
6 long aubergines
Sunflower oil, to fry

To garnish
1 large green pepper, cut into squares
1 medium tomato, cut into squares
Pinch of thyme

1 Melt the butter in a saucepan, add the lamb, onions and garlic, and cook over a medium heat, stirring occasionally for 10 minutes.

2 Add the tomatoes and chillies, and cook for a further 5 minutes until the meat is tender. Stir in the hot water and salt, cover and cook over a medium heat for approximately 1 hour, until the meat is tender.

3 Rinse and partially peel the aubergines in alternate lengthways strips. Remove and discard the stalks and cut each aubergine into six 1 cm (¾ in) thick lengthways strips. Place in a bowl and rub with salt to remove any bitter juices and leave for 25 minutes. Then rinse, dry and fry the strips in sunflower oil until golden brown. Leave to drain on kitchen paper. Preheat the oven to 200º C (400º F/gas 6).

4 Arrange six strips of aubergine diagonally in a small bowl so that each piece overhangs the bowl equally. Divide the meat into six equal quantities. Place one quantity of meat over the strips and fold over the overhanging aubergine strips to cover the meat. Carefully turn the bowl upside down onto an oven tray to form a dome. Repeat with the remaining ingredients. There should be six domes in total.

5 Garnish each dome with pepper and tomato squares placed on top of the dome and secured with a cocktail stick. Spoon over any remaining sauce and bake for 15 minutes. Sprinkle with thyme and serve hot.

Fried courgette balls

Kolokythokeftedes

SERVES 4–6
COOKING TIME: 25 MINUTES

500 g (1 lb 2 oz) potatoes
1 kg (2 lb 3 oz) onions, peeled
1 kg (2 lb 3 oz) courgettes, grated
120 g (4 oz) feta cheese, crumbled
1 tsp salt
Pinch of freshly ground black pepper
2 medium eggs, beaten
Plain flour, for coating the balls
Olive oil, for frying

1 Boil the potatoes and onions, then strain and chop into small pieces.

2 Combine the grated courgette, potatoes, onions, cheese, salt, pepper and eggs, and mix together to form a thick consistency.

3 Knead the mixture and shape into golf ball-sized balls. Coat each ball in flour and fry in olive oil until golden. Drain on absorbent paper and serve hot.

Fried potatoes with coriander

Batata bil kouzbara

SERVES 5
COOKING TIME: 30 MINUTES

100 ml (3½ fl oz) olive oil
1 kg (2 lb 3 oz) potatoes, peeled and cubed
2 garlic cloves, peeled
100 g (3½ oz) fresh coriander
2 Tbsp pine nuts
3 Tbsp dried coriander
1 Tbsp tomato paste
3 Tbsp lemon juice
Pinch of salt and freshly ground black pepper
½ tsp curry powder

1 Heat the olive oil in a pan and fry the potato cubes. Cook on a medium heat until golden brown, then drain on absorbent paper.

2 Crush the garlic with the fresh coriander and fry with the pine nuts in the same pan for 3 minutes until golden brown. Stir in the potato cubes, dried coriander, tomato paste and lemon juice. Season with salt, pepper and the curry powder. Simmer over a low heat for 3 minutes. Transfer to serving dish and serve immediately.

Stuffed mussels

Midye dolmasi

SERVES 10
COOKING TIME: 1 HOUR 35 MINUTES

40 medium mussels in shells
2 medium onions, peeled and finely chopped
½ tsp salt
½ tsp caster sugar
100 ml (3½ fl oz) olive oil
400 ml (14 fl oz) hot water
1 lemon, peeled and sliced

For the stuffing
130 g (4½ oz) white rice
2 Tbsp currants
100 ml (3½ fl oz) olive oil
100 ml (3½ fl oz) sunflower oil
2 Tbsp pine kernels
6 medium onions, peeled and finely chopped
1 tsp cinnamon
1 tsp allspice
1 tsp white pepper
1 tsp salt
1 tsp sugar
100 ml (3½ fl oz) hot water
½ bunch of fresh mint, chopped
Bunch of dill, chopped

1 Scrape the mussel shells with a knife or scrub with a brush. Soak in cold water while preparing the stuffing.

2 To make the stuffing, soak the rice in cold water for 30 minutes, then rinse thoroughly and drain. Soak the currants in warm water for about 15 minutes until they swell. Heat the olive and sunflower oils in a pan, add the pine kernels and onions, and brown slightly. Add the soaked rice and cook for 10 minutes. Then add the drained currants, spices, salt, sugar and hot water, and cook over a low heat for 15 minutes until the water has evaporated. Stir in the mint and dill, then set aside to cool.

3 Gently prise open each mussel with a knife without pulling the shells apart and remove the beard of the mussels, then rinse well and drain.

4 Place a tablespoonful of rice stuffing into each shell and close tightly.

5 Add the onions into a large pan and place a sheet of damp greaseproof paper over them. Arrange the stuffed mussels on top in layers and add the salt, sugar, olive oil and hot water.

6 Arrange the lemon slices over the mussels and place another sheet of damp greaseproof paper on top, weighted down with a plate. Cover and bring to the boil over a high heat for approximately 40 minutes. When most of the liquid has evaporated and the mussels are opened, place in a serving dish with the onions and garnish with the lemon slices.

Chickpeas in yoghurt sauce

Fattet el hommus bil laban

SERVES 4
COOKING TIME: 20 MINUTES

2 Tbsp butter
2 garlic cloves, peeled and crushed
1 tsp salt
1 Tbsp dried mint
400 ml (14 fl oz) plain yoghurt
1 tsp paprika
200 ml (7 fl oz) milk
4 pitta pockets
500 g (1 lb 2 oz) tinned chickpeas, rinsed
3 Tbsp pine nuts
1 Tbsp dried mint
1 Tbsp paprika

1 Heat the butter in a pan and fry the garlic with the salt and dried mint until lightly browned. Remove from the heat and transfer to a bowl. Strain the yoghurt and mix with the garlic.

2 Preheat the oven to 190º C (375º F/gas 5). Dissolve the paprika in the milk in a large bowl. Soak the bread in the milk for 30 seconds, then toast in the oven until brown. Break the toasted bread into pieces.

3 Arrange the bread in a shallow serving dish. Pour the yoghurt over the bread and top with the chickpeas. Sprinkle with the pine nuts, dried mint and paprika. Serve immediately.

Bean purée

Fava

SERVES 4
COOKING TIME: 1 HOUR

500 g (1 lb 2 oz) dried broad beans
2 tsp salt
2 Tbsp olive oil
Juice of 1 lemon
1 spring onion, finely chopped, to garnish

1 Soak the beans overnight in water. The following day, remove and discard the black tips and husks from the beans. Boil the beans in salted water for 30 minutes.

2 Strain the beans, place them in a saucepan and cover with water. Boil for a further 30 minutes, stirring regularly. Add the olive oil and lemon juice, and stir well. Transfer to a serving bowl and garnish with the chopped spring onion. Serve hot.

Cheese pies

Kallitsounia

SERVES 6
COOKING TIME: 40 MINUTES

For the dough
1 kg (2 lb 3 oz) plain flour
475 ml (16½ fl oz) water
1 tsp dried yeast
125 ml (4½ fl oz) olive oil
Juice of 1 lemon
1 tsp salt

For the filling
2 medium eggs, lightly beaten
2 kg (4 lb 6 oz) feta cheese, crumbled
Small bunch of mint, finely chopped
½ tsp crushed coriander
Salt and freshly ground black pepper

For the coating
1 egg, lightly beaten
1 Tbsp sesame seeds

1　Prepare the dough by mixing all the ingredients together in a bowl, then cover with a towel and set aside to rise in a warm place for approximately 1 hour.

2　In the meantime, make the filling. In a bowl, mix together all the ingredients.

3　When the dough has risen, roll it out to a 5 mm (¼ in) thickness and cut into 10 cm (4 in) circles. You will need 24 circles in total. Preheat the oven to 200º C (400º F/gas 6) and grease a baking pan. Place a spoonful of the filling into each of the dough circles and fold over to seal.

4　Glaze the top of the crescent-shaped parcels with egg and sprinkle with sesame seeds. Place on a baking tray and bake for 30 minutes or until golden brown.

Baked small fish
Bourtheto

SERVES 4–6
COOKING TIME: 25 MINUTES

1 kg (1 lb 3 oz) sardines or pilchards,
　rinsed and gutted
6 Tbsp olive oil
Pinch of salt and freshly ground black pepper
4 tomatoes, grated
1 onion, peeled and grated
Pinch of dried oregano
Small bunch of parsley, finely chopped

1　Preheat the oven to 190º C (375º F/gas 5). Drizzle half the oil over the fish and place in an oiled baking pan. Season with salt and pepper.

2　In a bowl, mix the remaining oil with the tomatoes, onion, oregano and parsley, and pour over the fish. Bake for 25 minutes. Serve hot.

Broad bean stew
Koukia

SERVES 4
COOKING TIME: 45 MINUTES

500 g (1 lb 2 oz) dried broad beans
125 ml (4½ fl oz) olive oil
2 onions, peeled and finely chopped
2 tomatoes, finely chopped
Small bunch of parsley, finely chopped
1 tsp cumin
4 bay leaves
Pinch of salt and freshly ground black pepper
475 ml (16½ fl oz) water

1　Soak the beans in water overnight.

2　The following day remove and discard the eyes (the black tips of the beans) with a sharp knife and boil the beans in water for 30 minutes, then strain.

3　Heat the olive oil in a saucepan and brown the onions, then add in the tomatoes, parsley, cumin, bay leaves, salt and pepper, and cook for 5 minutes.

4　Add the beans to the pan, along with the water, and simmer until the sauce thickens. Serve hot.

Moussaka

Mousakas

SERVES 6
COOKING TIME: 1 HOUR 45 MINUTES

4 Tbsp olive oil
1 kg (2 lb 3 oz) minced meat
2 onions, peeled and finely chopped
125 ml (4 fl oz) white wine
4 tomatoes, pulped
Salt and freshly ground black pepper
3 medium eggs, beaten
110 g (4 oz) feta cheese, crumbled
110 g (4 oz) breadcrumbs
1 kg (2 lb 3 oz) aubergines, cubed
1 kg (2 lb 3 oz) courgettes, cubed
2 Tbsp butter, for greasing

For the béchamel sauce
4 Tbsp butter
8 Tbsp plain flour
2 litres (4.2 fl oz) milk
30 g (1 oz) Parmesan cheese, grated
2 egg, yolks beaten
Pinch of salt, freshly ground black pepper
   and nutmeg

1 Heat the olive oil in a pan and fry the minced meat and onions until lightly browned. Pour in the wine, add the tomatoes, season with salt and pepper and cook for 30 minutes, stirring regularly. Then stir in the eggs, feta cheese and breadcrumbs.

2 In a separate pan, fry the aubergines and courgettes until lightly cooked.

3 Grease a 25 cm (10 in) square baking pan with the butter and alternate a layer of vegetables with a layer of meat. Repeat until the mixtures are finished. Preheat the oven to 190º C (375º F/gas 5)

4 To make the sauce, melt the butter in a pan. Remove from the heat and stir in the flour. Return to the heat, gradually adding in the milk and stirring all the while, and simmer for 9 minutes until thick. Add the Parmesan and egg yolks. Stir until thick, then remove from the heat and season.

5 Pour the sauce over the meat and vegetable mixtures and bake for 1 hour until golden.

Hot mezze   69

Octopus with wine and green olives

Htapodi krasato me prasines elies

SERVES 4–6
COOKING TIME: 35 MINUTES

125 ml (4 fl oz) olive oil
1 kg (2 lb 3 oz) octopus
125 ml (4 fl oz) red wine
Pinch of freshly ground black pepper
180 g (6½ oz) green olives, sliced

1 Remove and discard the ink sacs from the octopus and rinse thoroughly. Chop into pieces. Heat the olive oil in a pan and gently fry the octopus for 20 minutes

2 Add the wine and pepper, and simmer for 15 minutes until soft. Add a little water if necessary. Sprinkle with olives and serve immediately.

Mashed potatoes

Batata mahrouseh bil zeit

SERVES 4
COOKING TIME: 25 MINUTES

600 g (1 lb 5 oz) new or baking potatoes
100 ml (3½ fl oz) olive oil
2 onions, peeled and chopped
2 Tbsp dried parsley
Pinch of salt and white pepper

To garnish
Olive oil
1 tomato, sliced
Fresh mint leaves

1 Rinse the potatoes and boil in salted water until cooked. Drain and peel, then mash to a purée in a large bowl.

2 Stir in the olive oil, onions and parsley. Season with salt and pepper. Transfer the mashed potatoes to a serving dish. Drizzle with olive oil and garnish with the tomato slices and mint leaves.

Cabbage and rice pilaf

Lahanorizo

SERVES 4
COOKING TIME: 25 MINUTES

125 ml (4½ fl oz) olive oil
1 onion, peeled and finely chopped
1 small cabbage, chopped
475 ml (16½ fl oz) water
3 tomatoes, grated
425 g (15 oz) uncooked rice
Pinch of salt and freshly ground black pepper

1 Heat the olive oil in a large saucepan and fry the onion. Add the cabbage, stir, then add the water.

2 Add the grated tomatoes to the pan, stir and cook for 10 minutes. Finally, add the rice and, stirring occasionally, cook until the rice is cooked through and the water has been absorbed. Season with salt and pepper.

Stuffed courgette flowers

Anthi

SERVES 6
COOKING TIME: 40 MINUTES

40 courgette flowers

For the filling
3 tomatoes, grated
2 onions, peeled and finely chopped
125 ml (4 fl oz) olive oil
Small bunch of dill, finely chopped
Small bunch of parsley, finely chopped
Small bunch of mint, finely chopped
500 g (1lb 2 oz) white rice
Pinch of salt and freshly ground black pepper

1 Pick the courgette flowers fresh so they will be open. Rinse them, remove the stems and set aside while preparing the stuffing.

2 In a bowl add the tomatoes, onions, olive oil, dill, parsley, mint, rice, salt and pepper and mix together with 115 ml (4 fl oz) water.

3 Stuff the flowers with the mixture and place them in a pot. Cover with water and place a plate over them to stop the flowers from opening. Simmer until all the water has been absorbed. Serve hot.

Sis kebab with yoghurt

Yogurtlu sis kebab

SERVES 4
COOKING TIME: 1 HOUR 30 MINUTES

For the marinade
4 medium onions, peeled and finely chopped
4 garlic cloves, peeled and crushed
200 ml (7 fl oz) sunflower oil
1 tsp salt
Pinch of freshly ground black pepper

For the sauce
1 medium onion, peeled and finely chopped
1 garlic clove, peeled and crushed
2 Tbsp butter
2 mild green chillies, de-seeded and finely chopped
4 large tomatoes, peeled, de-seeded and diced
1 tsp salt

For the kebabs and sis kofte
1 kg (2 lb 3 oz) cubed lamb
1 green chilli, de-seeded and finely chopped
½ red pepper, finely chopped
1 small onion, peeled and finely chopped
2 garlic cloves, peeled and crushed
7 sprigs of parsley, chopped
Pinch of chilli flakes
½ tsp salt
Pinch of freshly ground black pepper
200 g (7 oz) finely minced lamb

1 Tbsp butter
3 small pitta bread
Pinch of salt
Pinch of sumac
1 tsp thyme
1 long aubergine
200 ml (7 fl oz) plain yoghurt

1 Start by preparing the marinade. In a large bowl, place the onions, garlic, oil, salt and pepper. Add in the cubed lamb and marinate overnight.

2 The following day, prepare the sauce. Heat the butter in a pan and lightly brown the onion and garlic. Add the chillies and stir for a few minutes, then add the tomatoes and salt, and cook over a moderate heat until soft.

3 Thread the marinated cubed lamb onto 8 skewers and set aside.

4 Prepare the sis kofte. In a large bowl, mix together the chilli, pepper, onion, garlic, parsley, chilli flakes, salt and pepper, then mix in the minced lamb. With wet hands squeeze an egg-sized portion of the mixture around a broad metal skewer, flattening and lengthening out. Repeat until all the mixture has been used.

5 Grill the skewers of cubed lamb and kofte under a medium heat until cooked, turning regularly to ensure all sides are evenly cooked.

6 Cut the pitta bread into small squares and lightly fry in the butter. Arrange in the centre of large serving dish and sprinkle with the salt, sumac and thyme. Spoon half of the tomato sauce over the pitta. Rinse and peel the aubergine in alternate strips, slice into rounds and fry until tender.

7 Beat the yoghurt and spoon over the pitta. Carefully remove the sis kofte from the skewers, cut in half and arrange with the meat skewers around the pitta. Arrange the aubergine rounds over the pitta.

Chickpeas in cumin and olive oil

Balila

SERVES 4
COOKING TIME: 40 MINUTES

400 g (14 oz) dried chickpeas, soaked overnight
in ½ tsp sodium bicarbonate

For the sauce
2 garlic cloves, peeled and crushed
100 ml (3½ fl oz) olive oil
1 Tbsp cumin
Pinch of salt

1 Rinse the soaked chickpeas and place in a pan. Cover with water and bring to the boil. Reduce the heat to medium and simmer for about 30 minutes, until cooked.

2 In the meantime, prepare the sauce. Mix the garlic with the olive oil, cumin and salt in a serving bowl. Drain the chickpeas and add them to the bowl. Mix well and serve immediately.

Chicken liver in pomegranate sauce

Kasbat el dajaj bi dibsil rouman

SERVES 5
COOKING TIME: 15 MINUTES

500 g (1 lb 2 oz) chicken liver
100 ml (3½ fl oz) olive oil
Pinch salt and freshly ground black pepper
50 ml (1¾ fl oz) lemon juice
1 Tbsp pomegranate paste

1 Trim any excess fat from the chicken liver and cut into cubes. Heat the olive oil in a pan and fry the livers until browned and almost tender. Season with salt and pepper.

2 Add the lemon juice and pomegranate paste to the pan, mix well and cook until the meat is tender. Transfer to a serving dish and serve immediately.

Stuffed kofte

Icli kofte

SERVES 8
COOKING TIME: 30 MINUTES

For the filling
2 Tbsp sunflower oil
1 kg (2 lb 3 oz) minced beef
1.5 kg (3 lb 5 oz) onions, peeled and finely chopped
1 tsp salt
1 tsp freshly ground black pepper
1 tsp red pepper
300 g (10½ oz) ground walnuts
300 g (10½ oz) blanched pistachio nuts

For the kofte
500 g (1 lb 2 oz) lean minced beef
3 medium potatoes, peeled and grated
2 Tbsp semolina
1 small onion, peeled and finely chopped
1 tsp salt
½ tsp freshly ground black pepper
½ tsp red pepper
400 ml (14 fl oz) water
1.5 kg (3 lb 5 oz) fine bulgur

Sunflower oil, for frying

1 Start by preparing the filling. Heat the oil in a pan and fry the minced meat until the juices have evaporated. Add the onions and cook for 5 minutes, then add the salt, black and red pepper, and nuts. Mix well and remove from the heat. Shape the mixture into finger shapes and set aside to cool.

2 To make the kofte, thoroughly knead together (or blend in a mixer) all the ingredients, excluding the water and bulgur, until a smooth dough is formed, then add the water and bulgur. Continue to knead the mixture in a bowl until it forms a paste.

3 Roll the kofte mixture into walnut-sized balls, hollow out the centres and stuff with the filling. You will need about 48 balls in total. Seal each hole by smoothing over with wet hands so there are no cracks. Place the balls under a damp cloth and when all are ready fry them in sunflower oil for 8 to 10 minutes, or until golden brown. Drain on kitchen paper and serve hot.

Stuffed vegetables

Gemista

SERVES 5
COOKING TIME: 1 HOUR 20 MINUTES

Vegetables for stuffing
5 tomatoes
2 aubergines
2 courgettes
2 red peppers
2 potatoes

For the filling
2 onions, peeled and finely chopped
125 ml (4 fl oz) olive oil
Small bunch of dill, finely chopped
Small bunch of parsley, finely chopped
500 g (1 lb 2 oz) white rice
Pinch of salt and freshly ground black pepper
3 tomatoes, grated
120 g (4 oz) feta cheese, crumbled

1 Preheat the oven to 190º C (375º F/gas 5). Hollow out all the vegetables for stuffing, set them aside and place their contents (except for the peppers) in a large bowl.

2 To make the filling, add the onions, half the olive oil, dill, parsley, rice, salt and pepper to the bowl and mix together.

3 Salt the hollowed insides of the vegetables and stuff them with the mixture. Place them in a deep baking dish.

4 Pour the grated tomatoes and remaining oil over the vegetables. Bake in the oven for approximately 1 hour 10 minutes. Sprinkle the cheese over the vegetables and bake for a further 5 minutes, or until the cheese melts. Serve hot.

Squid in lemon and coriander sauce

Sabbidej bahri

SERVES 6
COOKING TIME: 30 MINUTES

1 kg (2 lb 3 oz) squid
6 garlic cloves, peeled
200 g (7 oz) fresh coriander
Pinch of salt and white pepper
100 g (3½ oz) butter
200 ml (7 fl oz) lemon juice
Rind of 1 lemon
200 ml (7 fl oz) fish stock
Lemon wedges and coriander, to garnish

1 Clean the squids and cut into squares. Boil in salted water for 10 minutes, then drain and set aside.

2 Blend the garlic, coriander and salt in a food processor until smooth. Heat the butter in a saucepan, then add the garlic mixture with the squid squares. Fry for 5 minutes, then mix in the lemon juice, lemon rind and fish stock, and season with salt and pepper. Bring the mixture to the boil for 10 minutes.

3 Transfer the squids and sauce to a serving dish. Garnish with lemon wedges and coriander. Serve immediately.

Spicy potatoes

Batata harra

SERVES 4
COOKING TIME: 15 MINUTES

500 ml (18 fl oz) vegetable oil
1 kg (2 lb 3 oz) potatoes, peeled and cubed
1 Tbsp butter
85 g (3 oz) coriander
1 tsp chilli paste
Pinch of salt, freshly ground black pepper
   and paprika
Fresh coriander, to garnish

1 Heat the oil in a pan and fry the potato cubes until golden brown. Drain on absorbent paper.

2 Heat the butter in a separate pan and fry the coriander. Mix in the potatoes, chilli paste, salt, pepper and paprika. Transfer to a serving dish and garnish with fresh coriander. Serve immediately.

Fried kibbeh balls

Kebbeh maklieh

SERVES 4
COOKING TIME: 1 HOUR 15 MINUTES

For the stuffing

3 Tbsp vegetable oil
2 onions, peeled and finely chopped
200 g (7 oz) lean lamb, coarsely minced
1 cinnamon stick
Pinch of salt and white pepper
1 tsp sumac

For the meat shells

500 g (1 lb 2 oz) extra lean lamb from the leg, cubed
250 g (9 oz) brown burghul (cracked wheat)
Pinch of salt
½ tsp paprika
8 Tbsp iced water
Corn oil, for frying

1   Start by making the stuffing. Heat the oil in a pan and fry the onions until golden brown. Add the minced lamb and cinnamon stick. Cook until the juices have evaporated and the meat begins to brown. Season with salt and pepper. Remove from the heat and set aside. Discard the cinnamon stick and mix in the sumac.

2   To prepare the meat shells, divide the lamb into batches and process to a paste-like consistency using a food processor, then transfer to a large bowl. Add in the burghul, salt and paprika. Knead to a paste with moistened hands.

3   Process the mixture again in four batches, adding two tablespoons of iced water to each batch, until the paste turns smooth. Combine in a bowl and knead again for about 1 minute, with moistened hands.

4   Divide the meat mixture into 20 egg-size portions and roll into balls. Make a hole in each ball with your finger, then work around the hole, pressing gently until you have a thin, round shell. Fill each shell with one tablespoon of the stuffing, then gently close up the hole, again with moistened hands, and place on a tray. Larger quantities of kibbeh may be prepared in advance and frozen for a later use.

5   Heat the corn oil in a pan and deep-fry the kibbeh balls in batches until completely browned. Lift out with a slotted spoon and drain on absorbent paper. Serve immediately.

Chicken wings with coriander

Jawaneh el dajaj bil kouzbara

SERVES 4
COOKING TIME: 15 MINUTES

24 chicken wings
400 ml (14 fl oz) vegetable oil
4 garlic cloves, peeled and crushed
Bunch of coriander, finely chopped
1 Tbsp pomegranate paste
100 ml (3½ fl oz) lemon juice
Pinch of salt and freshly ground black pepper

For the garnish
Lettuce leaves
Fresh coriander leaves
Lemon wedges

1 Rinse the chicken wings in cold water and drain. Heat the oil in a pan and fry the wings in batches until golden brown and almost tender.

2 Mix in the garlic, coriander, pomegranate paste and lemon juice. Season with salt and pepper.

3 Transfer the chicken wings to a serving dish and drizzle with the cooking juice. Garnish with lettuce leaves, fresh coriander and lemon wedges.

Onion pie

Kremidopita

SERVES 6
COOKING TIME: 40 MINUTES

125 ml (4 fl oz) olive oil
1 kg (2 lb 3 oz) onions, peeled and finely chopped
500 g (1 lb 2 oz) feta cheese, crumbled
4 medium eggs, lightly beaten
Small bunch of dill, finely chopped
Salt and freshly ground black pepper
8 sheets filo pastry
Olive oil, for brushing the pastry

1 Preheat the oven to 190º C (375º F/gas 5). Grease a 25 cm (10 cm) square baking pan.

2 Heat the olive oil in a pan and fry the onions until lightly browned. Remove from the heat and add the feta, eggs, dill, salt and pepper and mix together.

3 Lay a sheet of filo pastry in the baking pan and lightly brush with olive oil. Then layer three more sheets of filo pastry overlapping and overhanging the first, each brushed with oil.

4 Spread the onion and cheese mixture over the pastry and fold the overhanging pastry over the filling, then brush with oil.

5 Layer the remaining four sheets of filo, each brushed with oil, over the mixture. Tuck the pastry around to seal the filling. Bake for 40 minutes or until golden. Once cooked, cut into squares and serve hot.

Cretan cookie

Sarikopites

SERVES 4–6
COOKING TIME: 10 MINUTES

For the dough
500 g (1 lb 2 oz) plain flour
200 ml (7 fl oz) water
3 Tbsp olive oil
2 Tbsp lemon juice or raki
1 tsp salt

For the filling
500 g (1 lb 2 oz) ricotta cheese

For the syrup
125 ml (4 fl oz) clear, runny honey
100 g (3½ oz) caster sugar
125 ml (4 fl oz) water

1 To prepare the dough, knead together the flour, water, half the olive oil, lemon juice or raki and salt.

2 Roll out the dough and cut into 10 x 20 cm (4 x 8 in) strips. You will need 20 strips in total.

3 Spread the ricotta cheese along the strips and twist each strip into a spiral, sealing at each end by folding over and smoothing water over the ends. Fry the strips in the remaining olive oil until golden brown, then drain and place in a serving dish.

4 To make the syrup, boil the honey, sugar and water for 5 minutes. Pour the hot syrup over the strips and serve hot.

TURKEY

Poached eggs with yoghurt

Cilbir

SERVES 2
COOKING TIME: 5–8 MINUTES

2 garlic cloves, peeled and crushed
4 Tbsp plain yoghurt
950 ml (33 fl oz) water
Pinch of salt
1 Tbsp white wine vinegar
4 medium eggs
1 Tbsp butter
Pinch of paprika
Bread, to serve

1 In a bowl blend together the crushed garlic and yoghurt.

2 In a large shallow saucepan bring the water, salt and vinegar to the boil, then lower the heat. Break one egg at a time into a bowl and slide carefully into the hot water making sure the eggs do not stick together. Cover and cook for 2 minutes.

3 When the whites have set and the yolks are veiled, carefully remove the poached eggs with a slotted spoon and place on a serving dish. Pour the yoghurt over the eggs.

4 Melt the butter in a small pan, stir in the paprika and pour over the yoghurt-topped eggs. Serve hot with bread.

Stuffed dumplings with yoghurt
Manti

SERVES 4
COOKING TIME: 30 MINUTES

For the pastry
300 g (10½ oz) plain flour
1 tsp salt
3 Tbsp olive oil
1 medium egg, beaten
4 Tbsp water

For the filling
200 g (7 oz) minced lamb
1 medium onion, peeled and grated
½ tsp salt
Pinch of freshly ground black pepper

For the tomato sauce
100 g (3½ oz) butter
3 medium tomatoes, peeled, de-seeded and diced
Pinch of salt
1 tsp chilli flakes
1 tsp dried mint

For the yoghurt sauce
3 garlic cloves, peeled and crushed
400 ml (14 fl oz) plain yoghurt

1   Start by making the pastry. Sieve the flour into a bowl, hollow out the centre and add the salt, olive oil, egg and water and mix together. Knead to a paste, cover with a damp cloth and set aside for 30 minutes. Then divide into two equal portions and place one under a damp cloth.

2   Flour a board, roll out one of the pieces to a 3 mm (¼ in) thickness, then cut into long 3 cm (1¼ in) wide strips, then cut into squares. Repeat with the other portion of pastry. There should be 80 squares in total.

3   To prepare the filling, mix together the lamb, onion, salt and pepper in a bowl. Place 1 teaspoon of the filling onto each square of pastry, gather the corners and fold into the opposite corners to form little parcels, sealing the corners with water.

4   Bring a pan of salted water to the boil and gently drop the dumplings in, one at a time, stirring occasionally to prevent them sticking together. Simmer for 15 minutes or until the parcels rise to the surface, then cook for a further 2 minutes. Remove from the heat with a slotted spoon, place in soup bowls and keep warm.

5   To prepare the tomato sauce, melt the butter in a frying pan, add the tomatoes and salt, and cook over a medium heat until softened. Just before removing from the heat, add the chilli flakes and mint, stir well and transfer to a bowl.

6   Prepare the yoghurt sauce. In a small bowl, stir the garlic into the yoghurt. To serve, spoon the tomato and yoghurt sauces over the dumplings and serve hot.

Sardines in vine leaves

Asma yapraginda sardalya

SERVES 10
COOKING TIME: 15 MINUTES

50 sardines
50 vine leaves

For the marinade
2 tsp salt
Juice of 2 lemons
1 tsp white pepper
600 ml (1 pint) olive oil

1 Keeping heads and tails intact, gut and remove the backbone of the sardines. Scrape off the scales, rinse well and drain, then place in a bowl.

2 Prepare marinade by mixing together the salt, lemon juice, pepper and olive oil, then pour over the sardines and set aside for 15 minutes.

3 In the meantime, scald the fresh vine leaves in boiling water, then dip in cold water to preserve their colour. If the leaves are preserved in brine, soak in warm water, then rinse thoroughly to remove excess salt before scalding.

4 Place each leaf on a clean surface, glossy-side down and veins facing upwards. Lay a sardine across the base of each leaf and roll up so that the head and tail stick out at either end. Brush each leaf with olive oil from the marinade.

5 Grill each leaf, starting with the flap side first, then turn over. Grill for approximately 7 to 10 minutes or until the leaves turn a yellowish-green colour. Place on a serving dish and serve hot.

Lebanese sausage in lemon sauce

Makanek

SERVES 4
COOKING TIME: 15 MINUTES

2 Tbsp vegetable oil
800 g (1 lb 12 oz) lamb or beef sausages
Juice of 1 large lemon

Heat the oil in a pan and fry the sausages on all sides for about 12 minutes. Pour in the lemon juice and cook for a further 3 minutes until tender. Transfer the sausages to a serving dish. Drizzle with the lemon cooking sauce and serve immediately.

Salads

Country salad

Choriatiki

SERVES 4

2 firm tomatoes, sliced
2 small cucumbers, sliced
1 green pepper, sliced
1 small onion, peeled and finely chopped
100 g (3½ oz) feta cheese, cubed
4 Tbsp olive oil
Pinch of salt
1 Tbsp white wine vinegar
1 tsp dried oregano
6 black olives

1   Place the tomatoes, cucumbers, pepper, onion and feta in a bowl and mix together.

2   In a separate bowl mix together the olive oil, salt, vinegar and oregano. Pour this mixture over the vegetables and garnish with the olives.

 LEBANON

Cabbage salad

Salatat el malfouf

SERVES 4
COOKING TIME: 15 MINUTES

For the salad
500 g (1 lb 2 oz) cabbage, chopped
4 sprigs of fresh mint, shredded
1 Tbsp dried mint
2 tomatoes, sliced

For the dressing
100 ml (3½ fl oz) lemon juice
200 ml (7 fl oz) olive oil
Pinch of salt and white pepper

1   Prepare the salad by mixing the cabbage with the fresh and dried mint and tomatoes in a large serving bowl.

2   To make the dressing, mix the lemon juice with olive oil and season with salt and white pepper.

3   Place the salad in a large serving bowl, drizzle the dressing over it and toss well before serving.

Bean salad

Fasulye piyazi

SERVES 6

500 g (1 lb 2 oz) haricot beans, soaked overnight
3 large tomatoes
2 medium onions, peeled and finely sliced
2 eggs, hard-boiled, chopped
6 black olives and a sprig of parsley, to garnish

For the dressing
125 ml (4 fl oz) olive oil
Juice of ½ lemon
Bunch of parsley, chopped
1 Tbsp white wine vinegar
Pinch of salt
½ tsp paprika

1 Rinse and drain the soaked haricot beans. Place in a pan, cover with water and bring to the boil. Simmer until the beans are tender, drain and cool, then place in a serving bowl.

2 Peel, de-seed and dice the tomatoes and add to the bowl, along with the onions and mix together.

3 Prepare the dressing by mixing together the olive oil, lemon juice, parsley, vinegar, salt and paprika, then pour over the salad. Garnish with the eggs, olives and parsley.

Thyme salad

Salatat el zaatar

SERVES 4
COOKING TIME: 10 MINUTES

400 g (14 oz) fresh thyme
2 small onions, peeled and sliced
400 g (14 oz) tomatoes, cut into wedges

For the dressing
1 garlic clove, peeled and crushed
50 ml (1¾ fl oz) lemon juice
100 ml (3½ fl oz) olive oil
Pinch of salt and white pepper

1 Rinse the thyme, pat dry and transfer to a large bowl.

2 Prepare the dressing by mixing the garlic with the lemon juice and olive oil. Season with salt and pepper. Drizzle the dressing over the thyme and toss well.

3 Transfer the thyme to a serving dish. Top with the onions and garnish with the tomato wedges.

Beetroot and cabbage salad

Salatat el chamandar wal malfouf

SERVES 4
COOKING TIME: 45 MINUTES

400 g (14 oz) beetroots
500 g (1 lb 2 oz) cabbage, finely chopped

For the dressing
2 garlic cloves, peeled and crushed
50 ml (1¾ fl oz) lemon juice
100 ml (3½ fl oz) olive oil
Pinch of salt and white pepper

1 Rinse the beetroots well, place them in a pressure cooker and steam for 30 to 45 minutes, until tender. Drain and rinse in cold water. Peel the beetroots and cut one into half circles and reserve for garnishing. Cut the remaining beetroots into medium-size cubes.

2 Prepare the dressing by mixing the garlic with the lemon juice and olive oil. Season with salt and white pepper.

3 Drizzle the dressing over the cabbage in a large bowl and toss well. Transfer the salad to a serving dish, then top the centre with beetroot cubes and garnish with the reserved half circles.

Lebanese salad

Salatat loubnanieh

SERVES 4

For the salad
4 cucumbers, sliced
2 tomatoes, cubed
6 spring onions, coarsely chopped
Small bunch of fresh watercress
Small bunch of fresh parsley
Small bunch of fresh mint
1 green pepper, cubed
1 lettuce heart, shredded

For the dressing
2 garlic cloves, peeled and crushed
50 ml (1¾ fl oz) lemon juice
100 ml (3½ fl oz) olive oil
Pinch of salt and white pepper

1 Prepare the salad by rinsing all the vegetables and green leaves. Drain well and transfer to a large bowl.

2 Make the dressing by mixing the garlic with the lemon juice and olive oil. Season with salt and white pepper. Drizzle the dressing over the salad and toss well.

Greek salad

Horiatiki

SERVES 4

3 Tbsp olive oil
1 Tbsp lemon juice
1 tsp dried oregano
Pinch of salt and freshly ground black pepper
4 tomatoes, sliced
1 onion, peeled and thinly sliced
1 cucumber, diced
125 g (4½ oz) feta cheese, cubed
16 kalamata olives

1 In a small bowl, mix together the olive oil, lemon juice, oregano, salt and pepper, and set aside.

2 In a separate bowl, mix together the tomatoes, onion, cucumber, feta and olives. Transfer to a serving bowl and pour the olive oil mixture over the salad and toss well.

Parsley salad

Tabouleh

SERVES 4
COOKING TIME: 15 MINUTES

For the tabouleh
400 g (14 oz) parsley, finely chopped
100 g (3½ oz) fresh mint, finely chopped
1 small onion, peeled and finely chopped
1 tsp salt
Pinch of freshly ground black pepper
50 g (2 oz) fine burghul (fine cracked wheat)
2 large tomatoes, seeded and finely chopped
Cabbage leaves, to garnish

For the dressing
100 ml (3½ fl oz) lemon juice
100 ml (3½ fl oz) olive oil
1 Tbsp lemon rind
Pinch of salt and white pepper

1 Rinse the parsley and mint and drain. In a small bowl, rub the chopped onion with the salt and black pepper and set aside.

2 Rinse the burghul and drain in a fine strainer, then transfer to a large bowl. Add the parsley, mint, tomatoes and onion to the bowl.

3 Prepare the dressing by mixing the lemon juice with the olive oil and lemon rind. Season with salt and white pepper. Drizzle the dressing over the salad and mix well. Transfer the tabouleh to a serving dish and garnish with cabbage leaves.

Shepherd's salad

Coban salatasi

SERVES 6

3 large tomatoes, peeled, de-seeded and chopped
3 mild green chillies
4 spring onions
4 sprigs of parsley
2 small cucumbers
8 black olives and 4 small chopped radishes,
  to garnish

For the dressing
125 ml (4 fl oz) olive oil
Juice of 1 lemon
1 Tbsp white wine vinegar
Pinch of salt and freshly ground black pepper

1 Place the tomatoes in a salad bowl. Finely chop the chillies, spring onions and parsley, and add to the bowl.

2 Peel and chop the cucumbers and mix in with the other ingredients in the bowl.

3 Prepare the dressing by mixing together the olive oil, lemon juice, vinegar and salt and pepper, then pour over the salad. Garnish with the olives and the radishes.

 GREECE

Beetroot salad

Patzarosalata

SERVES 4
COOKING TIME: 35 MINUTES

1 kg (2 lb 3 oz) beetroots
125 ml (4 fl oz) olive oil
3 Tbsp white wine vinegar
300 g (10½ oz) strained yoghurt
4 garlic cloves, peeled and crushed
90 g (3 oz) roughly ground walnuts
Pinch of salt

1 Boil, peel, then dice the beetroots. Place them in a serving bowl.

2 In a separate bowl, blend the olive oil together with the vinegar, yoghurt, garlic and walnuts. Pour this mixture over the beetroots. Add a pinch of salt, stir and chill before serving.

Pastries

Fresh oregano pastries

Fatayer bil zaatar

SERVES 5
COOKING TIME: 30 MINUTES

For the dough
600 g (1 lb 5 oz) plain flour
5 g (¼ oz) dry yeast
400 ml (14 fl oz) warm water
Pinch of salt

For the filling
100 g (3½) oz fresh oregano
2 Tbsp toasted sesame seeds
½ tsp sumac
100 ml (3½ fl oz) olive oil

1 Start by preparing the dough. In a large bowl, sieve the flour and hollow the centre. Dissolve the yeast in the warm water and add to the bowl along with the salt. Knead well until the dough is soft and springy. Cover with a damp cloth and set aside for at least 30 minutes until the dough has doubled in size.

2 To make the filling, mix the fresh oregano with the sesame seeds, sumac and olive oil.

3 Preheat the oven to 200° C (400° F/gas 6). Roll out the dough on a lightly floured surface to a 5 mm (¼ in) thickness, then cut into 10 cm (4 in) circles. There should be 40 circles in total.

4 Place one level tablespoon of filling on the lower half of each circle. Bring the top half over to cover the filling and pinch the edges firmly to seal. Arrange the pastries on a lightly greased baking tray and bake for 15 minutes.

Meat and pine nut pizza

Sfiha bil lahm

SERVES 5
COOKING TIME: 30 MINUTES

For the dough
400 g (14 oz) plain flour
85 g (3 oz) butter
Pinch of salt
5 g (¼ oz) dry yeast
200 ml (7 fl oz) warm water

For the filling
2 Tbsp butter
2 onions, peeled and chopped
2 Tbsp pine nuts
500 g (1 lb 2 oz) minced lamb
Pinch of salt and freshly ground black pepper
¼ tsp ground cinnamon
2 tomatoes, cubed

1 Start by preparing the dough. In a large bowl, sieve the flour and hollow the centre. Add in the butter and salt and knead well. Dissolve the yeast in the warm water and add to the bowl. Knead the mixture until the dough is soft and springy. Cover with a damp cloth and set aside for at least 30 minutes until the dough has doubled in size.

2 In the meantime prepare the filling. Melt the butter in a pan and fry the onions with the pine nuts until golden brown. Add in the minced meat and cook until brown and almost tender. Season with salt, pepper and cinnamon, then remove from the heat and leave to cool. Mix in the cubed tomatoes.

3 Preheat the oven to 200° C (400° F/gas 6). Roll out the dough on a lightly floured surface to a 5 mm (¼ in) thickness. Cut into 10 cm (4 in) circles. You will need 40 circles in total.

4 Place one level tablespoon of filling in the centre of each circle and bring up the edges together at four points to form a square. Pinch the edges together to seal the pies. Arrange on a lightly greased baking tray. Bake for 20 minutes, until golden brown.

Cheese pastries

Agnopites

SERVES 4
COOKING TIME: 15 MINUTES

For the dough
500 g (1 lb 2 oz) plain flour
200 ml (7 fl oz) water
3 Tbsp olive oil
3 Tbsp lemon juice or raki
Pinch of salt

For the filling
500 g (1 lb 2 oz) myzithra cheese,
  or any soft unsalted cheese
4 Tbsp milk

Olive oil, for frying
Honey, grape juice syrup, or sugar, to serve

1 Make the dough by mixing together the flour, water, olive oil, lemon juice or raki and salt. Knead well until a soft, springy dough is formed. Roll out the dough and divide it into small golf ball-sized portions.

2 Prepare the filling by mixing together the cheese and milk until smooth.

3 Make a small hole in each dough ball and fill with 1 teaspoon of the cheese mixture. Pull the dough over to seal the hole and roll the balls into 12 cm (5 in) circles with a rolling pin.

4 Fry the circles in olive oil until golden brown. Serve hot with honey, grape juice syrup or sugar.

Index